GREAT WARRIORS

VIKINGS

VALERIE BODDEN

CREATIVE EDUCATION

Published by Creative Education
P.O. Box 227, Mankato, Minnesota 56002
Creative Education is an imprint of The Creative Company
www.thecreativecompany.us

Design by Stephanie Blumenthal
Production by Christine Vanderbeek
Art direction by Rita Marshall
Printed in the United States of America

Photographs by Alamy (Mary Evans Picture Library, North Wind Picture Archives), Corbis (Ted Spiegel, Bo Zaunders), Dreamstime (Stasyuk Stanislav), Getty Images (Tom Dahlin, Michael Hampshire/National Geographic, STEFFEN ORTMANN/AFP, Popperfoto), iStockphoto (Dimedrol68, javarman3, Kamil Krawczyk, Andrew J. Shearer, Casper Wilkens), SuperStock (Stefan Auth/imagebrok/imagebroker.net, Bridgeman Art Library, Fine Art Photography Library, SuperStock, Universal Images Group)

Library of Congress Cataloging-in-Publication Data
Bodden, Valerie.
Vikings / Valerie Bodden.
p. cm. — (Great warriors)
Includes bibliographical references and index.
Summary: A simple introduction to the Scandinavian warriors known as Vikings, including their history, lifestyle, weapons, and how they remain a part of today's culture through books and films.
ISBN 978-1-60818-469-9
1. Vikings—Juvenile literature. I. Title.
DL66.B64 2013
948'.022—dc23   2012051835

First Edition
2 4 6 8 9 7 5 3 1

TABLE OF CONTENTS

Sometimes people fight.

They fight for food. They fight for land.

Or sometimes they fight for sport.

Vikings were warriors who fought

other people to steal treasure or land.

Vikings fought against many who did not want to give up their land

Vikings began fighting more than 1,200 years ago. They sailed from **Scandinavia** (*scan-duh-NAY-vee-uh*) to England, France, and other places in Europe (*YOO-rup*). They attacked **monasteries** and towns to steal jewels and money. They took people to sell as slaves, too.

VIKINGS SAILED IN BOATS CALLED LONGSHIPS
TO COUNTRIES NEAR AND FAR AWAY.

Vikings began to train when they were young boys. They climbed mountains and swam in cold water. They practiced using swords, spears, and bows. When a boy was 12, he could join a **raid**.

Vikings grew up with stories about warrior princesses called the Valkyrie

A Viking's favorite weapon was a long sword. The **hilt** of the sword was carved with words and pictures. Vikings also fought with bows and arrows, spears, and battle-axes.

VIKINGS WERE KNOWN FOR FIGHTING, BUT THEY ALSO
DECORATED THEIR SWORDS AND DRINKING HORNS (BELOW).

Vikings rode to battle on longships.

The ships were fast and easy to steer.

Vikings wore cone-shaped helmets

made of metal. They carried shields.

One large sail powered a Viking longship

When the Vikings got off their ship, they often began to fight. Sometimes people paid the Vikings with treasure to get out of fighting them.

THE PAYMENT VIKINGS REQUIRED IN RETURN FOR
NOT HARMING PEOPLE WAS CALLED DANEGELD.

VIKING FAMILIES IN
DENMARK LIVED IN
LONG, WOODEN HOUSES
SUCH AS THIS.

When a Viking trip was done, the warriors went home to their families. Many of them owned farms and slaves. Slaves took care of the farms.

Siegfried was a Viking leader who **laid siege** to the city of Paris. Sven Fork-beard was another Viking leader. He led many attacks on England. In 1014 A.D., he took over the country as its king. But he died a few weeks later.

Stories about Siegfried sometimes talk about another character named Gunnar

The Vikings fought for almost 300 years. But in the 1000s, many of them became **Christians**. They made friends with other Christian lands in Europe. So they stopped attacking those places. People kept telling stories about Vikings, though. Today, their stories live on in movies and books!

TODAY, PEOPLE DRESS UP AS VIKINGS AND
EVEN BUILD BOATS THE WAY VIKINGS DID.

Mar Atlantico

S. Canem

Brasil

Trapicus d

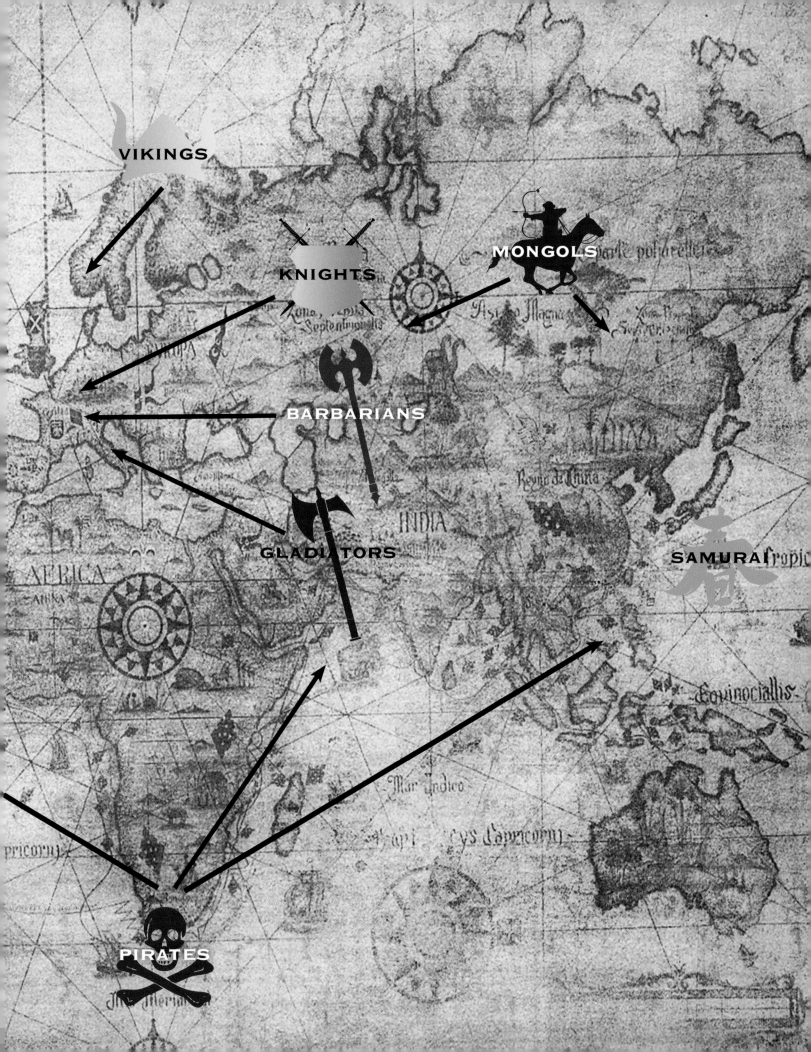

GLOSSARY

Christians—people who believe that Jesus Christ is the son of God

hilt—the handle of a sword

laid siege—attacked a placed by surrounding it and not letting food or other supplies into it

monasteries—buildings where monks (men who live as part of a religious group, away from other people) live

raid—a quick, surprise attack

Scandinavia—the part of northern Europe that includes the countries of Norway, Sweden, and Denmark

READ MORE

Hewitt, Sally. *The Vikings*. North Mankato, Minn.: Smart Apple Media, 2008.

Mulvihill, Margaret. *Viking Longboats*. Mankato, Minn.: Stargazer, 2007.

INDEX